I'm OK

by Paula Groothuis
Illustrated by Marian Pickman

Legwork Team Publishing
New York

Legwork Team Publishing
80 Davids Drive, Suite 1
Happauge, NY 11788
www.legworkteam.com
Phone: 631-944-6511

First published by Legwork Team 9/10/2008

ISBN: 978-1-6048-1278-7

Illustrated by Marian Pickman

Printed in the United States of America
Bloomington, Indiana

This book is printed on acid-free paper.

To my children, Julie and David

Acknowledgments
I am grateful for the love and
support of my family and friends
who have encouraged me to continue
to follow my dreams and to
become a published author.

Introduction

I'm OK reaches out to young people who so easily see the strengths of others, while failing to realize their own positive characteristics. It also offers a variety of language related to an assortment of activities. Paula has had more than twenty years of experience as a speech therapist, working with children who have found different aspects of learning to be a challenge. Her students' self-esteem issues have inspired her to write this book and to reach out to children to reassure them that they are "OK" just as they are.

There's a guy in my class—
his name is Paul.
Everyone looks up to him
'cause he's so tall.

And that's not all—
There's nothing he can't
do, with a basketball.

Every time Tommy has
a bat in his hands,
He hits the ball out
of the stands.

On the soccer field,
Joey is slick.
He never, ever
misses a kick.

When Mrs. Crabnose
teaches math every day,
Billy knows each answer,
right away.

Charlotte's her pet with her smile and tact.
In social studies, she never misses a fact.

Jennifer can dance
around the room with flair
And can kick her leg high
in the air.

In music Amanda has a very good ear.
Her voice sings out loud and clear.

Deanna's fingers
can move over the keys;
Playing piano, for her, is a breeze.

All the kids look up to Jim.
Whenever there's an election, they vote for him.

Give a pencil or crayon
or paintbrush to Bart,
And up on the wall goes
his creation in art.

15

When playing tennis,
Marylou wins every set.
The ball goes quickly over the net.

On the golf course, Georgie is the king.
He has a steady, powerful swing.
When he plays golf, he has lots of control.
The ball lands on the green,
right next to the hole.

They are more popular,
better looking, and brighter, you see;
More athletic, creative,
and stronger than me.
But I know I have qualities that are OK.
I tell the truth and do what I say.
I'm honest, I work hard, and I try my best.
Maybe I am just as good as the rest.

I never, ever call anyone names.
I share my toys and my computer games.
And Mom says that there is no end
To what I would do for a friend.

I have traits that make me fine.
You have yours, and I have mine.
It's who I am, not what I do
That makes me just as good as you!

Paula Groothuis is a speech therapist who lives and works on Long Island. She is the mother of two grown children, who are successful and "OK" in their own right. Paula previously published a compilation of personal poems entitled, A *Clearer Reflection*. Through the years, Paula found that the use of rhyme was a satisfying way to express her personal appreciation, gratitude, and birthday or anniversary wishes and was also hired to do the same for others. She has written poems for people throughout the United States and Canada, for such occasions as birth announcements, weddings, and retirements.

I'm OK...

For more information regarding Paula Groothuis
and her work, visit her Website:
www.PersonalizedPoemsByPaula.com.

Further copies of this book
may be purchased online from
LegworkTeam.com; Amazon.com;
BarnesandNoble.com; Borders.com
or via the author's Website,
www.PersonalizedPoemsByPaula.com.

You can also obtain a copy by visiting L.I. Books
or ordering it from your favorite bookstore.

Printed in the United States
125331LV00003BA